ABUNDANT WITH INTENTION

Powerful affirmations to navigate your life with purpose.

J.WHITE

Copyright © 2025 by J.White

All rights reserved. No part of this publication may be reproduced, distributed, or transmitted in any form or by any means, including photocopying, recording, or other electronic or mechanical methods, without the prior written permission of the publisher, except in the case of brief quotations embodied in critical reviews and certain other noncommercial uses permitted by copyright law.

ISBN: 979-8-218-78749-3 (Hardcover)

Emerald Gate Publishing
Englewood, CO | Newcastle, UK

Front cover image by S.J. Homestead
Printed by Emerald Gate Publishing, in the United States of America

First Edition 2025

INSIDE THIS BOOK:

Intention Setting Resources:
- Intention Setting Support Cycle™
- Three Steps Intention Setting Method™
- Four Phased Affirmations Approach™

Intentions: 16 carefully crafted affirmations for each intention that can be used to cultivate a daily practice. (256 in total) These can be used in chronological order or at random, for how they align with your life.

Intentional Activations: These are a variety of ideas, recipes and acts that foster a positive environment, which can enhance your experience when intention setting. The goal is to offer simple support to feel connected.

Bonus Meditations (4):
- Visualization
- Grounding
- Sensory
- Release

ABUNDANT WITH INTENTION

ABOUT THE AUTHOR

J. White is a Reiki Master, Energy Healer and Holistic Health Practitioner who centers her life around intention setting through the use of affirmations. On her personal journey, she created the methods used in this book: Intention Setting Support Cycle™, Three Steps Intention Setting Method™ and Four Phased Affirmations Approach™ to transform her life. In addition, she is an Intention Candle Curator for her renowned company Whitmark Co., which supports her mission to make intention setting and holistic health practices accessible to all communities.

ABUNDANT WITH INTENTION

DEDICATION

To everyone seeking purpose and abundance in your life: I see you with deep admiration. I appreciate your work. I offer you grace and honor your journey.

ABUNDANT WITH INTENTION

ABUNDANT WITH INTENTION

Introduction
What To Expect
For Your Reference
Affirmations:
  1. Intention
  2. Grounded
  3. Visualize
  4. Surrender
  5. Harmony
  6. Clarity
  7. Alignment
  8. Release
  9. Rebirth
  10. Protection
  11. Progress
  12. Resilience
  13. Empathy
  14. Gratitude
  15. Elevate
  16. Abundance
Onward (Conclusion)

YOUR JOURNEY STARTS NOW

ABUNDANT WITH INTENTION

I am abundant with intention. I have the innate and unlimited potential to live a life of purpose and alignment through deliberate actions every single day. I choose to live with intention. I trust that my intentions are rooted in values that are designed for good. I support my intentions with the time and energy I put in to uphold them. I live with intention, because I am my intentions.

ABUNDANT WITH INTENTION

ABUNDANT WITH INTENTION

INTRODUCTION

ABUNDANT WITH INTENTION

ABUNDANT WITH INTENTION

What does it truly mean to live with intention? The true meaning of living with intention is immensely personal, while it also holds universal impacts, all at the same time. In the literal sense, choosing to live with intention means one makes deliberate, mindful choices aligned with one's values and goals to move through the world in an authentic and positive manner. Rather than passively react to circumstances, living with intention allows for every action to be strung together with a level of accountability and deep connectivity according to a system of beliefs that each person holds. Three words to carry with you through this book are **deliberate, mindful,** and **choice**. Our actions must be deliberate in their timing and alignment, we must be mindful in such deliberation. And most importantly, every action on our journey comes down to a choice. By living with intention, you are choosing to equip yourself with the tools to align, adjust, and act according to your internal compass to guide you authentically on your journey. But, to understand that your choices hold the power, is critical on this path. Even in times when things are out of our control, there is a choice to be made on how to respond and how to move through the world. We always hold the power of choice.

ABUNDANT WITH INTENTION

Living with intention involves self-awareness, clarity, and the courage to make the choices that reflect our personal values. Rather than being swept along by timelines, obligations, or societal pressures, intentional living means asking, "Does this serve my purpose? Does this align with who I want to be?"

In theory, it sounds simple, but it is also easy to get distracted if you are not connected and consistent in your intentionality. Like all good things, this takes practice. We live in a world full of distractions, delusions, and constant need for external approval. Veering off course of our journey and compromising intentions may sometimes feel like the easier route. And one would argue that we live in a world where excuses are easier than accountability when taking such detours. And maybe that is true, but does short-term ease provide long-term fulfilment? I can stop you right there and tell you: no. Compromising your personal value system to appease the outside world or to obtain a fleeting and inauthentic high is a slippery slope. The strongest connection you should strive for on your journey is the one with yourself in a true and meaningful way, one that can offer you a sense of peace and pride. Living with intention is the purest act of self-love and self-acceptance you can offer. When you are in alignment, both mentally and physically, with your intentions, you will stand in your highest power. That in itself is a long-term, sustainable, and organic high that you won't come crashing down from.

Like all meaningful things, "Living With Intention" requires commitment and practice. How do you live with intention? I've learned that the practice of Intention Setting, specifically through the use of supportive affirmations, is a pathway to *living with intention* in the fullest sense. The practice of setting intentions allows intentionality to become a natural reaction and flows through your life with ease. When your intentions are in alignment with the way you move through the world, your spirit is lighter and your level of consciousness is abundant, making you a magnet to all that you are in alignment with. Affirmations are succinct, simple, yet positive statements that reflect a desired belief, mindset, or outcome. They are used as a tool to shift thought patterns, boost confidence, and reinforce a sense of agency over one's life. At their core, affirmations work by consciously choosing the language we use

ABUNDANT WITH INTENTION

with ourselves—replacing doubt, fear, or negativity with empowerment, clarity, and focus.

When integrated into daily routines, affirmations serve as mental anchors. Repeating phrases like "I am capable of handling what comes my way" or "I trust myself to make aligned decisions" helps reinforce those beliefs over time. This repetition can reshape neural pathways, making it easier to act in ways that align with your intentions, even when faced with challenges.

Affirmations are particularly powerful when paired with intention setting. Intentions are the "why" behind your actions—they reflect your core values and the energy you want to bring into your life. Affirmations help support these intentions by keeping them top of mind and energetically charged. If your intention is to live with more presence, an affirmation like "I choose to be fully here, in this moment" reinforces that goal each time you say or think it. By consistently using affirmations, you align your internal dialogue with your intentional goals, creating a bridge between mindset and action in reality. I will be honest, they don't magically solve problems, but they create fertile ground for intentional choices, helping you stay connected to what truly matters and grounded in the person you're becoming.

Setting intentions is a powerful, structured practice that allows you to begin and continue to create focus and alignment so that you can live with intention. This practice serves as a purposeful guide for both our thoughts and actions, thus creating our reality centered around our values. The beauty of intentions is the connection of our current self and our vision of our highest self. Instead of setting goals for "one day I will," we set intentions of "today I will be." or better yet "today I am." While goal setting is a plan to achieve something tangible, our intentions serve as a guide to our purpose in the current moment for both the tangible and intangible. Instead of making a list of things to do to achieve a goal, intention setting teaches us that everything plays a part in how we show up. When we act in accordance with the alignment of our values and intention we trust that we will stay on course to achieve all things. This shift in mindset is simple but impactful in the way we can live our lives in a more meaningful way and manifest our desires and potential in tangible ways. The art of speaking something into existence is exactly how intention setting acts as a conduit for ultimately living with intention.

When we are intention setting with the use of affirmations, these statements allow us to: **Slow Down. Simplify. Stabilize.**

First things first: Slow Down

Intention Setting, specifically through the use of affirmations, allows us as human beings to slow down. Yes, today's society wants everything fast. But it turns out that slowing down is the key to pure connection and stability. Anxiety, burnout, and depression are on the rise, and much of it can be traced to the relentless pace of modern life and over-connectivity. We are constantly overstimulated. This state of constant "on" leaves little room for our minds and bodies to rest or reset, never mind assess alignment with intentionality and purpose.

ABUNDANT WITH INTENTION

Let's talk through the science:

The autonomic nervous system has two main branches: the sympathetic (responsible for the fight-or-flight response) and the parasympathetic (which promotes calm and restoration). When stress hits, the sympathetic system floods the body with adrenaline and cortisol, preparing you for immediate action. This is useful in short bursts, but is damaging when activated constantly.

But the parasympathetic nervous system does the opposite—it slows the heart rate, lowers blood pressure, relaxes muscles, and supports digestion. In short, it helps the body return to a state of balance by its ability to slow down all functions. If we want to create a balance and alignment in our lives, slowing down, not speeding up, is the solution. When we choose to slow down, because remember: this is all a choice, it allows us the freedom and clarity needed to move intentionally. This ultimately gets us to our destination right on time, without unnecessary and damaging acceleration.

As we slow down, we possess the ability to quiet the

noise. In that silence, we create awareness and make it easier to identify a strong value system, reinforce patterns that support alignment, and in return, create a life of light and fulfillment, regardless of what we experience on our journey.

The next thing that affirmations do is simplify.

Affirmations are most powerful when they are simple because simplicity allows the mind to absorb and internalize the message easily and effectively. The human brain responds best to clear, concise language—especially when trying to shift deep-seated beliefs or rewire automatic thought patterns. A straightforward affirmation like "I am enough" is easy to remember, repeat, and believe over time. It doesn't get lost in complexity or vague ideas; it goes straight to the heart of the matter.

Simple affirmations also create less resistance. When a statement is too long, overly aspirational, or filled with abstract language, the mind may immediately question or reject it. In contrast, short, specific and clear affirmations are easier to accept as truth, even if only partially at first. They gently guide the mind towards a more supportive inner narrative without triggering skepticism or overwhelm. Less is in fact more!

Simplicity supports consistency. When an affirmation is easy to recall, it's more likely to be repeated throughout the day—in moments of stress, reflection, or decision-making. Repetition is key to making affirmations work, and simple phrases are much easier to integrate into daily life. Over time, these repeated messages begin to influence how we think, feel, and act—making it easier to stay aligned with our values and intentions.

Living with intention requires awareness, focus, and presence, all of which are nurtured by simplicity. When life is overcomplicated, it becomes easy to get distracted or pulled in directions that don't reflect your true values. But when you simplify your inner dialogue, specifically in how to connect through affirmations, you create room to pause, reflect, and act consciously in alignment.

ABUNDANT WITH INTENTION

Anchor it down with stability.

And finally, affirmations offer you stability in connecting your intentions to your actions in a foundation practice you can always return to reset. When life feels chaotic, stressful, or uncertain, a simple, grounding affirmation can serve as an anchor—a steady internal voice reminding you of your strength, worth, and direction. By consistently repeating affirmations that reflect your core values and inner truths, you create a foundation that remains solid even when external circumstances shift. Emotional stability comes, in part, from having consistent mental habits that support resilience by creating muscle memory. Affirmations can train the mind to focus on what's steady and empowering, rather than on fear or overwhelm. For example, an affirmation like "I am grounded, even in uncertainty" gently redirects your thoughts from panic or worry toward calm and centeredness. Over time, this repetition builds mental pathways that make it easier to access calm responses in stressful situations.

Affirmations also reinforce identity and self-trust, which are key to feeling stable in yourself. In

ABUNDANT WITH INTENTION

moments of doubt, repeating statements like "I trust that clarity will surface through my actions" or "I am safe and secure within myself," remind you of your own inner resources. This practice doesn't make problems disappear, but it helps regulate your emotional state so you can respond from a more grounded, intentional place.

In essence, affirmations provide a kind of emotional and mental foundation. They help hold you up when everything else feels shaky. Through daily repetition, they become a familiar rhythm in your mind—a quiet, steady presence that offers reassurance, focus, and stability when you need it most.

WHAT TO EXPECT

ABUNDANT WITH INTENTION

WHAT TO EXPECT

As we previously stated, affirmations are supportive statements to help elevate your intentions. The more you intention set and connect with your core values, the more natural intentional acts will become second nature to you in your day-to-day life, allowing you to live in your truth, align with your highest purpose, and (drum roll) live with intention. I tend to gravitate toward four categories of affirmations; thus, I created four affirmations of each category in the book to help support you on your journey. My process is to choose an intention and work through it as a step-by-step journey, four different ways with supportive affirmations. I do this in combination with the three-step process from the last section.

Let's do this together:

If my intention is "Present" I will begin with Reflection of what Present means in my life. I will then Align by establishing my why. I will Affirm, (here's where our affirmations can help you!) I will Honor with my three step intention process of Breathe, Ground and Visualize and finally I will Reflect to make it full circle!

WHAT TO EXPECT

Our affirmations are in the following categories: I choose, I trust, I support, and I am.

Only you will know which affirmation connects deeply with your intention-setting process. There are also no rules here, you can use one or four or all sixteen. My personal suggestion is to work your way through from I choose, next I trust, I support, and then I am. You can string them all together, or do it as a gradual process. Again, use your discernment, trust in your intuition, and allow yourself the space *and grace* to find your path.

Here is guidance on the four categories of affirmations you can find in this book:

I choose - Acknowledging that you choose this action. You are deliberate in this and have consciously made a choice that connects you with the intention. This acknowledgement shows that you have free will and the choice is yours, ultimately outlining that you can choose to live with pure intentions. You are the facilitator of all intentions. Without you, nothing is possible!

WHAT TO EXPECT

I trust - Acknowledging that you believe this intention will serve a purpose. You believe and put stock in the fact that this intention aligns with your values, and in return, those values serve a higher good.

I support - Acknowledging that you will put in the work to cultivate the results of this intention. This is your "how" and your accountability affirmation. In creating a supportive environment, as well as checks and balances will guide you in the right direction.

I am - Acknowledging that you are witnessing this intention in your current reality. Speaking this into existence with your full chest. It's not simply hoping it will happen, it's acknowledging this in the present tense to manifest it in physical form.

WHAT TO EXPECT

The Number 16

The number 16 carries various symbolic meanings across different cultures and belief systems. In general, it's associated with wisdom, insight, and spiritual connection, often signifying a breakthrough in consciousness.

The significance of 16 can be found in themes of finding your true life path, which is ideal when intention setting. Specifically, when we use the reductive methodology [from Numerology] of the number 16 (1+6), which is 7. The number 7 is also a highly spiritual number and is concerned with wisdom, spiritual awakenings, and seeking divine guidance in your everyday life.

The combination of vibrations found in the number 16 also has distinct and transformational energy. The presence of the number 1 marks new beginnings and a distinct time of growth. The number 6 is a sign of stability, home life, family life, balance, and leaning into symmetry. The presence of the number 7 can also serve as a reminder of the importance of making a connection to intuition and recognizing the power of

WHAT TO EXPECT

our mind. It's a profound invitation to know yourself better and to trust yourself on a much deeper level.

Just as intention setting transforms our psyche and allows us to awaken a spirit within us, the number 16 holds significance and support in the process. Each of the 16 intentions outlined in this book has 16 affirmations for you to use. Just as all elements of this book, the number 16 will guide us with intention and care on our journey.

WHAT TO EXPECT

What Are Intentional Activations?

Intentional Activations are a variety of ideas, recipes and acts that foster a positive environment, which can enhance your experience when intention setting. I found a deep connection in simple acts that connected me: mind, body, and spirit. More often than not, the smaller acts in life tend to hold the largest place in our consciousness. The goal here is to offer simple support that doesn't require a degree in rocket science to feel connected. It also validates my experience that it doesn't take an astronomical amount of money or expertise to support intention setting, but an open mind. These activations are accessible and simplistic enough in nature for everyone to take part in. In less than 16 minutes, you can commit to your intention with these suggestions to add intentionality to your practice. I don't claim to have created these concepts, but feel honored to align them with specific intentions and pass them along to you for your journey.

ABUNDANT WITH INTENTION

FOR YOUR REFERENCE

ABUNDANT WITH INTENTION

FOR YOUR REFERENCE

INTENTION SETTING SUPPORT CYCLE

> Intention Setting, specifically through the use of affirmations, allows you to slow down and quiet the noise around you. In that silence, create awareness, identify a strong value system, reinforce patterns that support alignment, and in return, create a life of light and fulfillment.

FOR YOUR REFERENCE

Reflect on what you value in a macro sense. Start broad and then narrow down a list of a few intentions that allow you to connect with those values. For example, I value connection and respect; therefore, my intention for the year is to be more present in my life so that I can truly experience deep connection and I do that by respecting the time and space of those around me, including myself. Daily, weekly, and monthly are common intention-setting timelines, but do whatever you are called to do and what feels most comfortable for you.

Align those values with a why. Understanding your why is so critical in connecting with your intention. This is where we remove the ego and focus on the why for our highest good, making the intangible tangible in our lives. It's also where we can see if our why is of value or simply a vanity metric. Why do I want to be more present? To deepen my connections with myself and those around me. In doing so, I can be more aware, more grounded, and focused. When I am focused, I am my best self.

FOR YOUR REFERENCE

Establish an affirmation that states and supports your intention, This is how you connect your why and add your how.

Affirmations are short, encouraging phrases delivered as a statement or proposition that is declared to be true. They are intended to be supportive and a beacon of guidance. This is where this book will come in very handy! I've realised that the affirmations are the most critical part in holding myself accountable and creating a solid foundation. I started by writing my intentions and affirmations at the start of the week and reviewing them at the end of the week. Continue to write and rewrite that affirmation (and/or speak them into existence) as frequently as possible. This practice helped me create a positive habit of repetition. I also repeat my affirmations during my morning and evening meditations. There's no exact science to this, so repeat, write, and speak your affirmations at a pace and frequency that works for you.

Honor Your Intentions: Create a ritual to honor your intentions. Make time each day, even if it's

FOR YOUR REFERENCE

just a moment, to create space to focus on your intention. If you're using intention candles, writing in your journal, or meditating - anything that speaks to you will do!

Reflect regularly on how your thoughts and actions align with your intention. You can journal or just take a quiet moment of reflection. Intention setting is a lifestyle and an ongoing journey. You won't be checking a box, but you will begin to see positive patterns of how you are living out your intentions.

FOR YOUR REFERENCE

THREE STEPS TO INTENTION SETTING

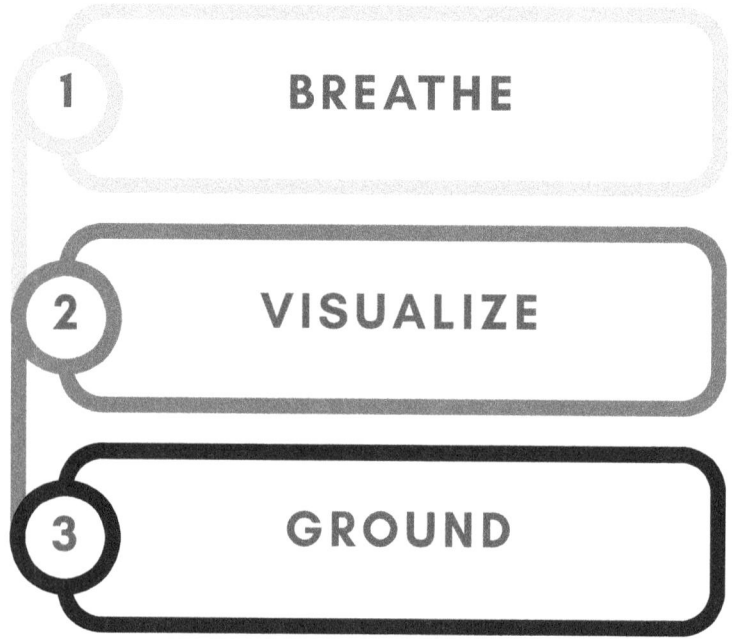

FOR YOUR REFERENCE

THREE STEPS TO INTENTION SETTING

How It Works:

1. Starting with a breathing pattern allows you to regulate your vessel and create a rhythmic tone to connect with your intention. This gives life to your experience.

2. When you consciously visualize your intention, you bring it to reality. When you see it in this phase, you will give yourself something to recognize in your daily life, thus living your intention.

3. This allows you to reinforce your connection with the Universe and create balance and stability in your practice both mentally and physically.

1
INTENTION

INTENTION

I choose my actions deliberately. I acknowledge and warmly embrace that every action I make is a choice; I hold that responsibility with the utmost regard.

INTENTION

The choices I make are a reflection of my spirit. I honor my spirit by moving through the world with intentionality. I connect my intentions with my values in every action.

INTENTION

I direct my energy with intentionality, knowing that where I place my energy and focus will multiply in perpetuity. I ask for the clarity needed to choose my actions wisely and respectfully for myself and those around me.

INTENTION

When I align my values with my actions, I am guided toward my highest power. When I choose intentionality, I choose to stand in my truth. Where there is truth, there is light.

INTENTION

I trust that my actions will align with my highest good and the values I hold. I ask that the Universe clear a safe and secure path for me to live with intention and lift the collective in doing so.

INTENTION

I trust that my actions are a reflection of my values and belief system. May my intentions guide me toward my highest self. May my intentions be pure and shaped in the light. May my intentions serve as an anchor for every move to create and continue alignment in everything I do.

INTENTION

I trust that my journey will be purposeful and lifted by my truth and existence.

INTENTION

I trust in myself, my abilities, and my commitment to my values, so that my intentions move through the world with clear meaning.

INTENTION

I support my intentions by holding myself accountable to truth, light, and free expression.

INTENTION

I create an authentic life supported by my intentions and in connection with who I strive to be in the world.

INTENTION

I support my intentions by diligence to my commitment to true connection that upholds my values.

INTENTION

I support my life with a solid foundation created in intention and purpose.

INTENTION

I am clear in my intentions. I am focused and connected to my values, creating meaningful action on my journey.

INTENTION

I stand in my highest power. I know that my journey is a series of choices that reflect my spirit. Each choice is a building block of power to shine my light out to the Universe.

INTENTION

I am living in my truth and believe each action is a meaningful expression of who I am. I honor myself and the collective by walking this path.

INTENTION

I am in control of my intentions and how they manifest in the world. I am responsible to give my values a voice on my journey. My intentions reflect the light only I possess.

INTENTIONAL ACTIVATION

Create A "Sacred Space"

Declutter - First and foremost, clearing a space of clutter clarifies the space, as we know everything holds energy. That makes space give it a protective environment. This is a space you'll continue to go back to, so a blank slate is the best way to start.

Find a Window - I like to have my sacred space by a window, for a variety of reasons. The most important being that the window can welcome in new fresh energy, even when it's not open. Given the practice of intention setting, I like the ability to welcome that energy in. It also serves as a great way to naturally charge my crystals and invite light into and on my space.

Crystals Curation - While I adjust what crystals are prominently displayed in my sacred space regularly, I do have my general "support system" of crystals available. Clear Quartz, Amethyst, Selenite, Obsidian. I always want this space to be clear, protective, and grounding to connect with my intentions. Those crystals are a wonderful foundation for how I move mind, body and spirit.

INTENTIONAL ACTIVATION

Create A "Sacred Space" continued

Journal Space – For me, a journal or something to write on a natural fit for a sacred space. I also keep a pen and some loose small pieces of paper that I place in my "intention jar." When it doubt write it out!

Supportive Items – Intention candles are wonderful supportive accents to your sacred space. You'll also commonly see affirmation cards, books that hold meaning to you, photographs, flowers and statues in a sacred space.

ABUNDANT WITH INTENTION

2
GROUNDED

ABUNDANT WITH INTENTION

GROUNDED

I choose to ground my energy with the strength of the earth beneath me. Each moment is an opportunity to stay connected and mindful.

GROUNDED

I am deeply connected to my core, even during emotional shifts. I choose to ground my energy. I allow myself to feel without losing my grounding. My emotional strength is anchored in peace and clarity.

GROUNDED

I choose to stay grounded and invite calm, centered, and peaceful energy to my journey so that I can connect to my highest purpose.

GROUNDED

I choose stability and security when I ground my energy and connect with the Earth. This act feeds my soul with purpose and truth.

GROUNDED

I breathe in stability and exhale tension. In each breath, I am deepening my roots and ground my spirit in divine connection with The Universe.

GROUNDED

I trust the energy I receive as I root myself deeply in my intentions. My foundation is strong, and I stand in my truth.

GROUNDED

I trust that when I am grounded, the Universe's energy can flow through me like a vessel of wisdom, peace, and light.

GROUNDED

I release emotional turbulence and embrace inner peace. My heart is grounded when I focus my energy on love and compassion for myself.

GROUNDED

I allow my body and mind to evolve with the seasons and cycles of life, while grounding my being in true faith on my journey.

GROUNDED

I support the act of grounding my connection with my intuition, allowing it to guide me on my journey forward.

GROUNDED

I am anchored in the present, I ground my being and release all worry as I grow with intention and purpose.

GROUNDED

I remove the energetic roots from all that no longer serves me. I ground myself in peace and a firm belief that I am worthy of feeling secure and safe.

GROUNDED

I am rooted in my intentions, and I stand tall, knowing I possess the stability to move through my journey confidently. I hold space for a deep and meaningful connection in this moment.

GROUNDED

I am one with the Universe. I am grounded knowing my intentions align with my purpose.

GROUNDED

I am grounded deeply within my truth and purpose. I am one with the Universe and easily adapt to any situation.

GROUNDED

I ground myself like the roots of a tree and allow my intentions to grow as firm branches. The firmer my foundation, the more abundance I shall receive.

INTENTIONAL ACTIVATION

Forest Bathing (Mindful Technique)

Forest Bathing, also known as (Shinrin-yoku), is a practice or process of therapeutic relaxation where one spends time in a forest or natural atmosphere, focusing on sensory engagement to connect with nature. This mindful practice helps to reduce stress hormones, lower blood pressure, and promote relaxation, which in turn helps to ground and center. Being in nature encourages a sense of presence and calm, fostering a deeper connection with the Earth and oneself. As a result, forest bathing can restore balance, enhance mental clarity, and reinforce a feeling of stability and rootedness as a whole.

This is not an exercise to rush. While taking a brisk walk, or running outside is a great form of grounding, Forest Bathing is an art of slowing things down so you can mindfully connect in a different way with the outdoors through observation and gratitude.

INTENTIONAL ACTIVATION

Forest Bathing (Mindful Technique)

Use this method to slow down your pace and connect with the outdoors to facilitate grounding.

5 things you can see.
4 things you can touch.
3 things you can hear.
2 things you can smell.
1 thing you can taste.

ABUNDANT WITH INTENTION

3

VISUALIZE

ABUNDANT WITH INTENTION

VISUALIZE

I choose to only see myself in all my potential. As I visualize my highest self, I open my senses to this experience. My entire body is consumed with this experience.

VISUALIZE

I choose a path of abundance. As I visualize myself in this state, I ask the Universe to provide me the necessary tools and guide me toward this reality.

VISUALIZE

I choose to only see myself in my fullest potential and power. As I witness this visualization, I allow myself to open up to the miracles of the Universe.

VISUALIZE

As I visualize myself, I choose to connect with all the emotions of achieving this life. I see, I feel, I become.

VISUALIZE

What I see becomes my reality. I clearly and fully visualize the prosperity and abundance I desire in my life. I hold space for gratitude and growth as I watch this story unfold in real time.

VISUALIZE

When I visualize a life with intention and purpose, I raise my vibration levels and trust that this attracts positive energy into all areas of my existence.

VISUALIZE

I trust that what I see is my reality. I trust in my ability to manifest greatness and welcome abundance into my life.

VISUALIZE

I firmly believe in what I see for myself. I manifest these visions to become my reality.

VISUALIZE

I welcome a clear vivid picture of my journey. As I watch this vision in front of me, I manifest it into reality. What I see, I believe.

VISUALIZE

I allow myself to visualize all the abundance I dream of. I see myself in real time. I open my consciousness to be gifted with the tools to make this vision a reality.

VISUALIZE

I see myself as a free-flowing being. I allow myself to release all negative blockages and see myself surrounded by light.

VISUALIZE

When I visualize a life with intention and purpose, I raise my vibration levels and attract positive energy into all areas of my existence.

VISUALIZE

I have the ability to see and fully witness myself live the life of my dreams.

VISUALIZE

I see myself in all my power. I open my consciousness to capture this visualization and carry it with me on my journey.

VISUALIZE

I witness myself achieve my goals and walk my path with ease. I take intentional and deliberate action to make this my reality.

VISUALIZE

I visualize what is meant for my intentions to actualize. I am attracting my desired reality into my life.

INTENTIONAL ACTIVATION

Turmeric Bath Soak for Visualization

Turmeric is a powerful addition that supports both emotional and physical health. Turmeric's active compound, curcumin, helps improve mood by relieving stress and negative thoughts, while facilitating positive energy. Curcumin works by increasing levels of dopamine and serotonin, which are neurotransmitters that regulate mood, making it a phenomenal support herb for visualization!

This quick and easy recipe for a Turmeric Bath Soak can help connect with your intention to visualize:

- **Raw Turmeric Powder - 1 Tablespoon**
- **Dry Lavender Buds - 1 Tablespoon**
- **Himalayan Sea Salt - 2 Tablespoons**
- **Coconut Oil (Melted if raw) - 1 Teaspoon**

Mix in a bowl evenly and disperse in the hot bath. Soak for 15-20 minutes, preferably before bed, as the experience will support your body in a relaxed state. *Take a turmeric bath before bed will also help support your dream state to continue your visualization process overnight as well.*

INTENTIONAL ACTIVATION

Why a bath: A hot bath can serve as a powerful tool for mental clarity that allows the mind to slow down and release stress. The warmth of the water helps relax tense muscles, creating a sense of physical ease that can translate into mental relaxation.

Additionally, the sensory experience helps reset energy levels by stimulating circulation and promoting the release of endorphins. This boost in circulation awakens the mind, leaving you feeling more alert. The tranquil environment and heat encourages deep breathing, which increases oxygen flow to the brain and further enhances mental clarity and energy. Overall, a hot bath acts as both a physical and mental reset, fostering clarity, relaxation, and a fresh start.

ABUNDANT WITH INTENTION

4

SURRENDER

SURRENDER

I choose to surrender to the unknown. I release my need to control, knowing that all that will be is as it should be.

SURRENDER

I choose to do my part, and trust that the Universe will provide the rest and align my journey as it should be.

SURRENDER

As I completely surrender, I trust that everything is unfolding as it should with divine timing and in full alignment with my intentions.

SURRENDER

I choose to release all resistance.
I welcome the lessons and growth
that come when I surrender.

SURRENDER

I confidently believe in divine timing. I know that my timing will align with my soul's journey.

SURRENDER

I embrace the uncertainty and trust that the right opportunities will arrive right on time.

SURRENDER

I have unwavering trust in the unfolding of my life's path and highest purpose. I surrender, so the Universe can serve my favor without worldly resistance.

SURRENDER

I release my attachment to specific outcomes and know that when I surrender, I am open to unexpected blessings.

SURRENDER

I fully place my faith in the divine timing of my manifestations. I surrender to the flow of abundance, knowing that all I seek with arrive when I effortlessly let go and let be.

SURRENDER

I surrender the need to rush my story. I let go of the past and embrace the opportunities of the future with open arms.

SURRENDER

I embrace the flow of the Universe. I am a magnet to the energy I release. I surrender control and in doing so, my true abundance will arrive right on time.

SURRENDER

I connect to my own inner authority and power. I surrender all expectations and use that energy to align my purpose through my actions instead of control.

SURRENDER

I surrender to the journey ahead of me. I find peace in knowing that I am exactly where I need to be at all times.

SURRENDER

When I surrender, I show up in my life with an open heart and an open mind to all the blessings available to me.

SURRENDER

As I surrender, I step forward in faith and light.

SURRENDER

I surrender to this very moment. I choose harmony between myself and the Universe. When we are in harmony, I can walk my journey to my highest purpose.

INTENTIONAL ACTIVATION

Progressive Muscle Relaxation

Set aside 15 to 20 minutes for PMR. Find a quiet, comfortable area and be sure to turn off your phone to avoid distractions. Avoid holding your breath, which can cause more tension. Inhale deeply when you tense your muscles and exhale fully when you relax. Move in a sequence that works for you. For example, you can start at your head if you want to, and move down your body.

- Start by lying or sitting down. Relax your entire body. Take five deep, slow breaths.
- Lift your toes upward. Hold, then let go. Pull your toes downward. Hold, then let go.
- Next, tense your calf muscles, then let go.
- Move your knees toward each other. Hold, then let go.
- Squeeze your thigh muscles. Hold, then let go.
- Clench your hands. Pause, then let go.
- Tense your arms. Hold, then let go.
- Squeeze your buttocks. Pause, then let go.
- Contract your abdominal muscles. Pause, then let go.

INTENTIONAL ACTIVATION

Progressive Muscle Relaxation (continued)

- Inhale and tighten your chest. Hold, then exhale and let go.
- Raise your shoulders to your ears. Pause, then let go.
- Purse your lips together. Hold, then release.
- Open your mouth wide. Hold, then let go.
- Close your eyes tightly. Pause, then release.
- Lift your eyebrows. Hold, then release.

ABUNDANT WITH INTENTION

5
HARMONY

ABUNDANT WITH INTENTION

HARMONY

I choose harmony and peace. I am fully capable to return to a place of peace and calm regardless of what is put on my path.

HARMONY

I choose the energy and flow in my life. By design, my default is harmony by offering the Universe and myself love, compassion and grace.

HARMONY

I attract balance and harmony into my life with every decision I make.

HARMONY

I choose harmony in the face of fear. Harmony is my power and I embrace it with every breath.

HARMONY

I trust that prioritizing harmony and peace will always keep me safe and secure.

HARMONY

I trust that everything in and around me is in perfect harmony.

HARMONY

I trust that harmony exists even in the unknowns of life. I trust that when I surrender to the flow of harmony, peace will fill my soul.

HARMONY

I will not force anything in my life. I trust that harmony surrounds me and provides me all that is meant for me on my journey.

HARMONY

I create and preserve the harmony around me by seeking out the light in all situations I may face.

HARMONY

Harmony is always welcome in my life. May peaceful and calm energy always outweigh negative energy.

HARMONY

Harmony nurtures my life and supports the alignment of my path with clarity and purpose. Harmony strengthens and centers my life.

HARMONY

The more harmony I bring into my life, the stronger my relationships will be with others, with myself and my purpose.

HARMONY

I am a vessel of peace and harmony flows through every part of my being. My mind, body and spirit are in divine balance.

HARMONY

Harmony is my natural state. I am in tune with the divine frequency of harmony in all that I do.

HARMONY

I am in sync with the harmony within. I honor that rhythm and allow harmony to intentionally guide my journey.

HARMONY

I am in sacred harmony with my purpose. I am surrounded by peaceful energy and allow that to direct my life.

INTENTIONAL ACTIVATION

Rose Water

There is a long tradition of rose water being used in holistic medicine to support your emotion state as far back as the 7th century. The steaming of rose water has been traditionally used as a way to improve a person's mood. You can also simply drink it as well! Research has shown that rose water has antidepressant and anti-anxiety properties that can treat a number of mental conditions, including: depression, grief, anxiety and tension. This is also a great option for treating migraines and headaches by put it on a cloth and places it on your forehead, similar to the use of lavender.

To make rose water, simply rinse fresh rose petals, add them to a pot of distilled water, simmer on low heat for 30-45 minutes, then strain the liquid into a bottle; you can use this as a calming mist on your face, wrists, or pillow!

INTENTIONAL ACTIVATION

Rose Water Tips:

- **Quality of roses:** Opt for organic roses whenever possible to avoid chemical residues.
- **Distilled water:** Use distilled water to ensure the purest form of rose water.
- **Storage:** Keep your homemade rose water in the refrigerator for up to a week

ABUNDANT WITH INTENTION

6
CLARITY

ABUNDANT WITH INTENTION

CLARITY

I choose to be clear and level-headed. When I choose clarity, I release myself from unnecessary roadblocks and limitations.

CLARITY

Clarity is a form a peace. I welcome ultimate clarity to receive the lessons and better shape my future to live with full intention, as my best self.

CLARITY

I choose clarity over comfort. I acknowledge this choice allows me to learn and live in connection with the truth.

CLARITY

I choose to be clear in my focus and choose to remove anything from my life that prevents me from living with full mental clarity. When I am clear, I invite light into my life.

CLARITY

I have a clear vision of my future that is intentional and full of light. I trust my ability to use that clarity to align each step of my journey with purpose.

CLARITY

I trust in the power of clarity. It will clear the path ahead of me and allow me to travel in light and purpose

CLARITY

I trust that I will always receive clarity in times of chaos. That clarity will center me and align my actions with my intentions.

CLARITY

I trust that the clarity provided to me is always right on time and right in message. I allow myself to be open to new insights that will better my journey.

CLARITY

As the veil is lifted, the clarity revealed is for my own good. I use this information to release what is not serving me and create new paths with alignment and purpose.

CLARITY

A clear mind is the foundation to a meaningful life. It sets the tone for truth and acceptance. When my mind is clear, all things are possible.

CLARITY

I remove all distractions and noise that surrounds me, so that I can approach each day with clarity and alignment.

CLARITY

I vow to learn from the areas of my life that I now see clearly, so that I can grow and evolve with intention.

CLARITY

I am clear and focused on my intentions. Every decision I make is rooted in clarity and wisdom to connect with my highest self.

CLARITY

My intuition is clear and provides me with stability and decisive action to move through the world with intention.

CLARITY

When my mind is clear, the path forward is visible and the terrain is always manageable. Clarity guides my road.

CLARITY

I am in touch and in tune with my own intuition. Answers are beginning to materialize with complete clarity in my mind. I now have a clear vision of what I desire to manifest into reality.

INTENTIONAL ACTIVATION

Magnesium Butter

Magnesium supports mental clarity by regulating neurotransmitters and maintaining healthy brain function. It helps balance levels of glutamate, a key neurotransmitter involved in learning and memory, while calming excessive neural activity that can lead to brain fog or anxiety. Adequate magnesium levels support synaptic plasticity, which enhances the brain's ability to adapt, process information, and retain knowledge efficiently. This makes it an essential mineral for maintaining focus, clear thinking, and mental sharpness throughout the day.

Additionally, magnesium helps reduce stress and improve sleep quality—two factors that significantly impact cognitive clarity. By moderating the stress response, magnesium can ease mental tension and improve overall mood and cognitive function.

INTENTIONAL ACTIVATION

Magnesium Butter

The key to clarity is rest and destress to have a clear mind. This is something easy and affordable that you can make in the comfort of your own home to support rest and clarity in your life.

Dissolve (pure) magnesium flakes in boiling water, then slowly add the mixture to melted shea butter. Blend until smooth, then refrigerate for 1-2 days and then leave at room temp.

- For anxiety, you can apply magnesium body butter to your heart chakra to provide a sense of clam and root you in clarity.
- You can also apply it to the bottoms of your feet and calves to help with sleep.
- Lather on stiff joints and sore areas before bed to allow your body to relax and cultivate a full night sleep to wake up refreshed and clear.

ABUNDANT WITH INTENTION

7
ALIGNMENT

ABUNDANT WITH INTENTION

ALIGNMENT

I choose to act in alignment with truth and light. I vow to use the knowledge I have to honor my intentions and the greater good.

ALIGNMENT

Every decision of my life brings me closer to my purpose and divine alignment.

ALIGNMENT

I choose to remove all distractions and negative energy from my life to prioritize genuine alignment.

ALIGNMENT

I choose alignment knowing that it will allow me access to my highest power.

ALIGNMENT

I allow my intuition to guide me, as I hold myself accountable to align with my intentions.

ALIGNMENT

I have the divine ability to easily seek and step into opportunities and energetic experiences that align with my mission.

ALIGNMENT

I walk my journey in alignment, trusting that connection will honor my purpose and bear abundance in my life.

ALIGNMENT

My actions, my thoughts and my values are in harmonious alignment. I turn within and listen to my intuition to guide my path.

ALIGNMENT

I effortlessly align my mind, body, and spirit by prioritizing my intentions and focusing my thoughts on purpose.

ALIGNMENT

I take full responsibility to maintain alignment in my life. I have the power to create boundaries to protect my alignment by design.

ALIGNMENT

Peace fills my spirit when I choose what feels in alignment to my soul.

ALIGNMENT

With each day, I invite the connection needed to align me emotionally, spiritually and energetically.

ALIGNMENT

My life is in perfect alignment with my intentions. I feel secure in knowing that I act in deliberate and methodical ways that guide my journey.

ALIGNMENT

I am an aligned being. I allow the Universe to use my connection as a conduit for light in the world.

ALIGNMENT

I am in alignment to attract abundance and energy that supports my soul's mission.

ALIGNMENT

I am in alignment. Each step of my journey is greeted with intention, light and harmony with my purpose.

INTENTIONAL ACTIVATION

Box Breathing - Rhythmic Focus for Alignment

Box breathing, also known as square breathing, is a deep breathing technique that can help calm the nervous system and reduce stress. It involves inhaling, holding, exhaling, and holding again, each for a count of four, like tracing the sides of a box.

How to do box breathing:
1. Inhale: Breathe in slowly through your nose for a count of four.
2. Hold: Hold your breath for a count of four.
3. Exhale: Breathe out slowly through your mouth for a count of four.
4. Hold: Hold your breath again for a count of four.
5. Repeat: Repeat this cycle for a few minutes or as long as needed.

INTENTIONAL ACTIVATION

Mindfulness Breathing - Emotional Alignment

Mindfulness breathing is a simple yet powerful technique that involves focusing your attention on your breath to cultivate awareness of the present moment. It's a form of meditation that helps calm the mind and body by noticing the natural rhythm and sensations of breathing without trying to change it.

How to do mindful breathing:
1. Here's how to practice mindful breathing:
2. Find a comfortable position: Sit or lie down in a way that allows you to relax your body.
3. Focus on your breath: Pay attention to the sensation of your breath as it enters and leaves your body. You might notice the air moving in and out of your nostrils, the rise and fall of your chest or belly, or the feeling of the breath in your throat.
4. Don't judge or change your breath: Simply observe your breath without trying to control or alter it.
5. Gentle redirection: If your mind wanders, gently bring your attention back to your breath.

INTENTIONAL ACTIVATION

Heart Centered Breathing - Gratitude Alignment

Heart-centered breathing is a technique that involves focusing your attention on your heart area while breathing slowly and deeply. It's a simple yet powerful tool for self-regulation, stress reduction, and improving emotional well-being. By consciously connecting with your heart and breathing deeply, you can shift your emotional state, enhance focus, and promote a sense of calm.

Here's how to practice heart-centered breathing:
1. Find a comfortable position: Sit or stand with your back straight.
2. Bring your attention to the area of your chest where your heart is located.
3. Visualize the breath entering and leaving your heart space.
4. Breathe deeply and slowly: Inhale for a count of 5 seconds and exhale for a count of 5 seconds.
5. Hold a positive emotion: As you breathe, try to evoke a feeling of appreciation, care, or love.
6. Continue for a few minutes: Practice for at least one minute, or longer if you find it helpful.

8
RELEASE

RELEASE

I receive a newfound freedom in the act of release. I end attachments to patterns, behaviors and individuals that no longer serve me. I choose my highest purpose over all.

RELEASE

I am choose to break down the barriers in my life, one by one. I allow myself to experience my feelings as I release all connection to past barriers and create a new path for my future.

RELEASE

I release the grip of emotional weight, I choose peace. I allow positive energy to flow through me and create space to expand my consciousness and usher in light.

RELEASE

I release the past and welcome the limitless potential of the future. Focusing my energy on the present and the future is a conscious choice to honor my well-being, growth and light.

RELEASE

Trusting the Universe liberates me from worry and fear. I release my control to gain the highest power.

RELEASE

I am empowered as I release all blockages and negative energy. I trust and embrace the light to fill those spaces.

RELEASE

The Universe has a divine plan for me. Every release creates space for cosmic blessings to enter my life in accordance with that divine plan.

RELEASE

I trust that when I release, I create space for something great to unfold. Release is not a loss, but an act of self love to align my journey.

RELEASE

I release what no longer serves me. I let go of the past and embrace the present. I release all resistance and embrace the flow of life with full intention.

RELEASE

I offer this practice to find peace and release all patterns that no longer serve me. I honor all emotions that surface in this process, knowing they are guiding me to my divine purpose.

RELEASE

I gracefully release the chains of the past from my life, allowing space for new meaningful connection and direction. The past is a closed chapter.

RELEASE

I release control and trust that what the Universe delivers will always be in alignment and honor my highest good. Letting go aligns me with the natural flow of divine blessings.

RELEASE

I release the past and walk to the future securely. I create and maintain a protective barrier for all that does not align with my energy and intentions. I am safe and protected.

RELEASE

When I release, I create a heartfelt opening for new blessings to enter my energetic space. Without release, I cannot receive.

RELEASE

I release the worries that bind me to the past. I am braver with each step I take. The less I control, the more I attract. I am on a journey of growth, authenticity and abundance.

RELEASE

I am free to move forward in my life. I let go of all that ties me to the past and carry the lessons to support my future.

RELEASE

I live with ease. I live with peace. I live with intention – all because I am committed to release all that no longer honors my spirit.

INTENTIONAL ACTIVATION

Cord Cutting for Release

One of the most powerful intentions is the act of release. As we explore our journey, we evolve, we change, and must release that which no longer serves us in order to step into our highest self. There are also times when it's less about letting go of a "thing" or a "person" and more of letting go of habits, emotions, and patterns that are tying you to a lower vibration. When we choose to release, we create space for all that aligns with the now.

Things You Need:
- Candles: Symbolizing illumination and transformation.
- Crystals: Suggestions are black obsidian, amethyst, clear quartz, or selenite, to absorb and transmute negative energy.
- Sage and Palo Santo: For cleansing the energy. Palo Santo provides an extra layer of protection.
- A Pair of Scissors: To physically represent the act of severing the cords.
- String of any kind to support the visualization of tied cords, I recommend twine.

INTENTIONAL ACTIVATION

Cord Cutting for Release

1. **Clear and Protect Your Energy:** Before beginning the ritual, light the sage or Palo Santo and allow the smoke to envelop you and your surroundings. As you do so, set the intention to release any negative energy that may be present. Then begin to state the focus of your release. It can be a person, a situation, an emotional attachment, a feeling, anything you need to let go of.
2. **Visualize The Ties**: Close your eyes once and visualize the cords that you yearn to release, granting them the spotlight in the forefront of your consciousness. Everything you seek to release is represented in a cord now.
3. **Cut The Cords:** With a pair of scissors, begin the physical act of cord cutting with the twine. As you do this, repeat out loud or to yourself: "I release all that no longer serves my highest good. I am free." As you cut each cord, imagine it dissolving into light and energy, leaving you feeling lighter and more liberated. Trust the process:you are releasing these attachments with love and compassion for yourself and others involved.

INTENTIONAL ACTIVATION

Cord Cutting for Release

4. Seal With Satisfaction: Repeat this cord-cutting affirmation

"I now sever and release any and all energetic cords that do not serve my highest good. I release you and I release me from these binds. All cords are destroyed, across all dimensions, times and planes, never to return again. I hereby banish these energetic cords and recover now all energy that was once lost."

5. Hold Space for Gratitude: Take a moment to pause with a grateful heart as you begin a new journey without cords of what tied you to negative elements of your life.

ABUNDANT WITH INTENTION

9
REBIRTH

REBIRTH

I choose to welcome in a new version of myself with open arms. I shed my old self to grow and evolve.

REBIRTH

I choose to release the past and welcome new beginnings with an open heart.

REBIRTH

I choose a new chapter filled with hope and possibility. I release all chains of the past and choose a new road to walk.

REBIRTH

I choose transformation. I choose to renew my sense of self and allow myself to start a new: mind, body and spirit.

REBIRTH

I trust that the changes in my life are leading me to a brighter future. I welcome in this new cycle with clarity and pure energy.

REBIRTH

I trust that my spirit and highest self will emerge in this next phase of my journey. I embrace each cycle of my life with gratitude and compassion.

REBIRTH

I trust in the cyclical journey of my life. I trust that in my rebirth I am gaining a renewed spirit that can soar to my highest potential.

REBIRTH

I trust that my spirit and highest self will emerge in this next phase of my journey. I embrace each cycle of my life with gratitude and compassion.

REBIRTH

I let go of what no longer serves me and embrace what's to come. I am open to the possibilities that come with new beginnings.

REBIRTH

My journey of rebirth is a path to greater self-discovery and growth. I commit to my intentions to usher in the next cycle as the best version of myself.

REBIRTH

I walk forward with an open mind for the next chapter of my life. I ask that this next journey be aligned with my purpose, abundant in wisdom and anchored in love.

REBIRTH

I allow myself the ability to release and rise. I will hold the past with gratitude for the wisdom. I will embrace this rebirth in alignment with my intentions.

REBIRTH

I am ready to rise from the ashes of the past and walk a new path. Every ending is a new opportunity for a fresh start.

REBIRTH

I am reborn with a renewed sense of purpose and strength. This change brings me closer to my true self and my highest potential.

REBIRTH

I am empowered to reinvent myself and align my life with light. I release fear and step confidently into my new reality.

REBIRTH

I am closest to my purpose when I embrace all the seasons of my journey. I vow to constantly evolve and let go of what no longer serves me so that I may live in light.

INTENTIONAL ACTIVATION

Immunity Tea Recipe

There's something special about ginger root when working through a rebirth; it has this fiery, earthy energy that feels like it can burn away the old and make space for the new. When you sip on fresh ginger tea it's like telling your body, "Hey, let's clear out what's not serving us." It warms you from the inside out, waking up your system and setting a tone of renewal, like your cells are being gently nudged back into alignment.

Mentally, ginger has this sharp, invigorating quality that helps clear the fog. It's stimulating without being overwhelming, bringing clarity and focus, especially when you're trying to break free from old thought patterns or start a new chapter.

Spiritually, ginger carries an ancient, healing energy that connects you to your intuition. Incorporating ginger into your daily ritual, like a cup of tea, can feel like a gentle but powerful reset. It's a way of saying, "I'm ready to shed what's old and step into what's next."

INTENTIONAL ACTIVATION

Immunity Tea Recipe

- Peeled fresh ginger root
- 1 cup water
- 1/2 lemon
- Dash cayenne

1. Peel and chop ginger into chunks. For 1 cup, aim for about 1 heaping Tbs. You want to slice it up so the properties of the ginger will seep into the tea.
2. Bring water to a boil Pour the hot water over the ginger pieces, which you've placed at the bottom of a large mug.
3. Let it sit for at least 2 minutes, the ginger and hot water should be cooled down enough. At that time, squeeze half a lemon into the tea.
4. Give at least one good shake of cayenne pepper right into the tea. If you can handle spice, like me, you can try 2 shakes! *Don't overdo it*

ABUNDANT WITH INTENTION

10
PROTECTION

ABUNDANT WITH INTENTION

PROTECTION

I choose safety and stability by protecting my peace and energy above all else.

PROTECTION

I choose to prioritize my safety by living my truth and connecting with my intentions so negative energy cannot enter my space.

PROTECTION

I choose to be vigilant and aware of my surroundings, so that I only welcome light on my journey.

PROTECTION

I choose my own well being and that inner peace creates an unbreakable protection and emotional security.

PROTECTION

I trust when I create clear boundaries I am protected and fully aligned with my intentions on my journey.

PROTECTION

The universe is my shield,
guarding me against all
negativity.

PROTECTION

My strength comes from within, and I trust that I am always protected by the loving energy of the Universe.

PROTECTION

I trust my intuition will always guide me to safety. I welcome love and protection to surround me on my journey.

PROTECTION

I create a shielding barrier of protection to deflect any negative or unwanted energy from taking up space in my presence.

PROTECTION

I honor my own boundaries, standards and intentions. This serves as a means of protection for any low vibrations that I encounter.

PROTECTION

I walk through life confidently, knowing that I am protected. I am connected to the universal energy of safety and peace.

PROTECTION

My spiritual strength protects me from harm; everything happening is for my highest good. When I am in alignment with my true self, the energy of peace and protection surrounds me.

PROTECTION

I am divinely protected and guided at all times. I release all negative energy and invite positivity into my life.

PROTECTION

I am in control of my energy and only allow positive energy to enter my space. I am full protected by any energy that does not align with my journey.

PROTECTION

I am safe and protected from all that does not serve me. I am shielded from harm and negativity.

PROTECTION

I am surrounded by a protective light of love. My spirit is strong and secure in its journey. The Universe ensures my path is safe and clear.

INTENTIONAL ACTIVATION

Fire Cleansing Technique

Fire cleansing is one of the most powerful energy cleansing rituals as it involves one of the most potent elements. Fire is one of the most respected in the spiritual and energetic world due to its enormous capacity to purify and protect. Fire, in combination with herbs, neutralises energies, breaks any bad vibrations and destroys all kinds of energetic stagnation in your home.

Fire cleansing is something important, yet simple, that you can do regularly for energetic purity. It's often used in a seasonal cadence, much like spring cleaning. When our energy and intentions are protected, we create a space of peace in our environment that allows us to step into our highest self without barriers.

Suggested items:
- White Sage
- Dried Rosemary
- Palo Santo
- Frankincense

INTENTIONAL ACTIVATION

Directions:

1. In a burn-friendly bowl, add your ingredients.
2. Open all windows and doors to allow the energy to move through and out.
3. Start at the front door and move clockwise through each room, wafting the smoke into corners, closets, and other areas where energy might accumulate. Visualize the smoke carrying away negativity and filling the space with positive energy.

ABUNDANT WITH INTENTION

11
PROGRESS

ABUNDANT WITH INTENTION

PROGRESS

I choose to move forward towards progress in my life. Forward motion, even the smallest step is a meaningful act of progress. I celebrate each act and honor its contribution to my journey.

PROGRESS

My progress is unstoppable and in full alignment with my intentions. I choose take deliberate action to move forward and create a clear path infront of me to continue my progress in meaningful ways.

PROGRESS

I acknowledge that progress is an individual standard. I choose to focus on my own journey and embrace my path forward as it is unique to my experience.

PROGRESS

I choose progress in my life. I commit to evolve as I grow and learn, so that I can continue to be a positive energy for change in the world.

PROGRESS

I trust that the small, consistent actions are the foundation for the progress I seek to achieve on my journey.

PROGRESS

I have the power to create the life I desire. Progress is achieved one step at a time. I remain patient with myself as I grow and evolve.

PROGRESS

The timing of my journey does not define me. I will trust the process and celebrate myself for all progress. I am putting forth a genuine effort and recognize that that is enough.

PROGRESS

I trust that even when I cannot see it, I am progressing towards my highest self. Every step of my journey is a valuable contribution to this evolution.

PROGRESS

I persist until I succeed. Every step of my journey is a form of progress to evolve into my highest self and serve my highest purpose.

PROGRESS

I welcome the next evolution of my life. I seek forms of progress and growth to enhance my life and align me with my highest power.

PROGRESS

The progress I make today will shape the abundance and alignment I enjoy tomorrow.

PROGRESS

I honor the path forward toward progress by channeling confidence and strength on the forged path. I release myself of the fears of the unknown and welcome the future with an open heart and mind.

PROGRESS

I am making consistent progress, no matter how small the steps. Every day, I am becoming the best version of myself.

PROGRESS

I am ready to progress today. I will rise to every occasion and move my intentions forward with commitment and integrity.

PROGRESS

I am a product of progress. As I grow and evolve on my journey, progress leads me to my highest self.

PROGRESS

I am progress. My intentions allow me to facilitate growth and I use all the knowledge I am given along the way to continue to move forward in divine time.

Small Wins Progress Jar

Each day, I take a small piece of paper and write a victory achieved that day. It does not have to be a major win; in fact, it should be small incremental victories that are documented. I fold up the paper and put it in a glass jar. At the end of the month, I pour the jar out to see how far I've come. I read those victories with gratitude and to marvel in the progress I've made. This is a beautiful reminder of the small steps that often get overlooked that contribute to forward progress in large, visible ways. Each step is important, and we must not let them get lost in the shuffle.

INTENTIONAL ACTIVATION

It's easy to overlook the little wins, especially when we're focused on big goals or waiting for a major breakthrough. But documenting those small victories—like getting up on time, choosing nourishing food, setting a boundary, can actually build serious momentum. When you write them down or take a moment to acknowledge them, you're sending yourself a powerful message: "I'm moving forward." That steady recognition creates a sense of trust in your own process, which is essential when you're setting and living with intention.

Those tiny wins stack up and remind you that your intentions aren't just abstract ideas floating out there—they're becoming real through deliberate action. It helps reframe the journey. You're not starting over every day—you're building on what you've already done, no matter how small it seems.

Documenting victories trains your mind to look for what's going right, not just what's missing. That shift alone can energize your intentions. You start moving from pressure into presence and purpose.

ABUNDANT WITH INTENTION

12
RESILIENCE

ABUNDANT WITH INTENTION

RESILIENCE

I choose to face life's challenges head on and rely on my resilience to guide me on this journey with courage and grace.

RESILIENCE

Regardless of circumstance, I choose resilience. No matter how many times I get knocked down, I will rise triumphantly and energetically to serve my highest good.

RESILIENCE

Even in the darkest of times, I can find strength and resilience within myself to keep going. I am stronger than anything I have to go through.

RESILIENCE

I choose to walk my path with resilience. I choose to remain committed to my purpose and persevere through every challenge I face.

RESILIENCE

I trust in my ability to overcome obstacles; my resilience guides me intentionally on my journey.

RESILIENCE

Every challenge on my journey strengthens my resolve and resilience. I emerge from difficult situations stronger than before and continue to rise with higher purpose.

RESILIENCE

I trust that I am going in the right direction and my resilience will serve as my guide and light the path I walk ahead.

RESILIENCE

I trust the strength of my mind. I trust the resilience of my heart. I trust my alignment to my intentions. I trust that I am greater than any challenge that comes my way.

RESILIENCE

My resilience keeps me grounded and focused. This is a gift that allows me to overcome challenges with courage and stamina.

RESILIENCE

I hold gratitude for the resilience within that fires my spirit confidently for every twist and turn of this journey. Throughout the uphill climbs and bouts of adversity, the Universe intuitively navigates my journey with integrity.

RESILIENCE

I am capable of handling anything that life throws at me because of my resilience. I turn every setback into an opportunity for growth and learning. The power of my soul rises above any hurdle I have to face.

RESILIENCE

My resilience allows me to adapt in the face of challenges. I grow and learn from every experience, no matter how difficult. I remain calm and centered, even in chaotic times.

RESILIENCE

I am powerful, capable, and resilient. I have the ability to face my journey with strength and courage.

RESILIENCE

I am resilient in the face of life's uncertainties. I rely on my inner wisdom and strength to move forward.

RESILIENCE

I am resilient in my pursuit to make my dreams a reality. I take intentional steps each day and face each obstacle with courage and commitment to my vision.

RESILIENCE

I am a beacon of strength and resilience. I embrace my inner power and let it shine. I am the warrior of my own life. I am resilient and shall always overcome.

INTENTIONAL ACTIVATION

Five R's of Resilience

Regulation - It is important to steward the body, heart and mind in order to strengthen our parasympathetic nervous system—the system that controls the body's ability to relax. Attend to and nurture yourself physically and emotionally by: Calming and grounding in the here and now, and allowing time to recover from any stress.

Reflection - When we regulate our emotions with healthy reflection, we are then able to reframe our minds and live in truth. I journal for this "R" to help process my thoughts. I will write down which emotions are tied to whatever is holindg me back in the past, not allowing me to move forward. Then I ask myself what outside influences contributes to my feelings. How much of that do I know to be with one hundred percent certanty. I'll begin to noticing the assumptions made about certain situations, and identifying the "lies believed" about myself and others. Relfection also offers a place where you an honor yourself and the path you've walked. It helps to redirect our path, but give credit to the past as well without remaining there.

INTENTIONAL ACTIVATION

Five R's of Resilience

Relationship - Social support is critical in building resilience. Connection with community, in any way that fits your lifestyle will provide a postive reinforcement of care.

Rest and Removal - Intentionally making time to rest, and remove yourself from the negative space creates a cadence of reset. This does not have to be long periods of time, even dedicating 5-10 minutes of rest can support resilience.

Reason - Identifying your why allows you a clear purpose that evokes resilience on your journey. When you have a why that is intentionally connected to your spirit, anything is possible, and resilience is almost innate. This connection to why, ties back to our four types of affirmations as well: I choose, I trust, I support, I am. So when you identify your why. You choose to honor "your why"; You trust "your why" is in alignment with your highest good. You support "your why" with resilient efforts. And then you are your why!

ABUNDANT WITH INTENTION

13
EMPATHY

ABUNDANT WITH INTENTION

EMPATHY

I choose empathy when I receive and respond to the emotions of others, especially those emotions in which I have no experience first hand.

EMPATHY

I choose to be empathetic with everyone I interact with. I am open to learn from situations and emotions I have not experienced by honoring those who have with belief and understanding.

EMPATHY

I choose to release all judgment and approach all situations with empathy and light in order to cultivate genuine connection.

EMPATHY

I choose to appreciate the unique experiences of all those I encounter. I believe in the power of empathy to bridge gaps and promote harmony.

EMPATHY

I trust who I am and who I choose to be. I know that my empathy creates a safety of inclusiveness and understanding for the greater good.

EMPATHY

I trust that empathy will guide my journey and create growth in my emotional intelligence to serve my highest purpose.

EMPATHY

I trust that genuine empathy can serve as a guiding light to provide genuine interactions with others on my journey.

EMPATHY

I trust that the information I learn from empathy will shape my journey to align with my intentions and bring me to my highest purpose with genuine connection.

EMPATHY

I am open to learning from the experiences of others. I create an environment where empathy is valued and practiced in all interactions.

EMPATHY

I allow myself to see things from another person's perspective clearly when I lead with empathy and compassion.

EMPATHY

I strive to see the world through the eyes of those I interact with. I treat others with kindness and empathy, even in challenging situations.

EMPATHY

I seek an empathetic approach in my life, not to fix the situation at hand, but to support those who have experienced it with love and understanding.

EMPATHY

I am empathetic. Through both my words and actions, I will support and uplift others with empathy and encouragement.

EMPATHY

I am a compassionate and empathetic person. I listen with the intent to understand. I offer support and comfort to those in need.

EMPATHY

I am committed to living a life of empathy.
I am patient, understanding and respect the feelings and experiences of others.

EMPATHY

I am a source of compassion and empathy. My heart is open to the suffering of others. I am a force for good in the world.

INTENTIONAL ACTIVATION

Mindful Consciousness for Empathy

The process of being mindful without judgment can allow individuals to face negative thoughts or emotions without reacting to them automatically.

Find a quiet space: Close your eyes (optional): This can help you further minimize distractions and focus on your auditory senses.

Tune into the sounds: Begin by noticing the most prominent sounds around you. Then, gradually expand your awareness to include more subtle sounds.

Don't judge: Simply observe the sounds without labeling them as good or bad, pleasant or unpleasant.

Acknowledge distractions: If your mind wanders, gently bring your attention back to the subtle sounds. If you are having difficulty bringing your mind back to center, focus on your breath and exhale audibly in a cycle of 5-6 times. Focus on the audible exhale as a reset and start again.

INTENTIONAL ACTIVATION

Mindful Consciousness for Empathy

Reflect: After a few minutes, take some time to reflect on your experience. What sounds did you notice? How did they make you feel? What do those feelings mean to you?

You can use this exercise of reflection as a sounding board when trying to relate with empathy in external situations. Having the ability to identify emotions, name them, and appreciate their experience contributes to empathetic thinking in a meaningful way that honors the experience.

ABUNDANT WITH INTENTION

14
GRATITUDE

ABUNDANT WITH INTENTION

GRATITUDE

Gratitude is the lens through which I choose to see every moment. No matter the circumstance, I find something to appreciate, and that energy transforms my life.

GRATITUDE

I make the conscious choice to begin and end each day in gratitude, anchoring my life in its alignment. With this mindset, I attract more to be grateful for.

GRATITUDE

I choose to carry gratitude in my heart like a compass. When I am grateful, I gravitate toward peace and alignment.

GRATITUDE

I choose gratitude not as a reaction, but as a way of being. When my heart is grateful, I honor and recognize that life itself is a gift.

GRATITUDE

Through gratitude, I release resistance and embrace acceptance. I trust that everything is happening for my growth and highest good. I practice gratitude in all moments of life.

GRATITUDE

When I speak words of gratitude into existence, the Universe responds in kind. I trust that my energy attracts experiences that reflect my grateful heart and in return I am rewarded with blessings of abundance.

GRATITUDE

Gratitude is my foundation, and it grounds me in the truth of my blessings. Even in uncertainty, I seek gratitude to guide the path ahead.

GRATITUDE

I trust that gratitude will allow me to see and embrace lessons in challenges and struggle. With gratitude, all things are possible. I thank the Universe for all that I am and all that I will be.

GRATITUDE

Gratitude shifts my focus from lack to fullness. What I have is enough, and from this place of contentment, miracles unfold in abundant measures.

GRATITUDE

Gratitude connects me to the present and awakens my spirit to the blessings of now. This moment is a gift, and I receive it fully with an open heart.

GRATITUDE

Every breath I take is an act of gratitude for the life flowing through me. I honor the sacredness of being alive.

GRATITUDE

Gratitude brings light to my darkest days. It's the quiet strength that helps me rise again with hope and an open heart.

GRATITUDE

I am grateful and I expand beyond limitations. Gratitude creates a cycle of value in my life that directs on journey in an intentional way.

GRATITUDE

My gratitude turns ordinary moments into sacred ones. I am in tune with the frequency of the present moment and an enlightened perspective to honor each moment of my journey.

GRATITUDE

Gratitude is my daily practice, and it elevates everything I encounter. I am a powerful force of transformation through the grateful energy in my life.

GRATITUDE

Gratitude keeps me rooted in joy and appreciation. It is my constant, my anchor, and my power. When I am grateful for my journey, I hold a deeper understanding of my experiences.

INTENTIONAL ACTIVATION

10 Gratitude Journal Prompts

1. List 5 everyday items you are grateful for, things that make your life easier.

2. List 3 people who you are grateful for and why.

3. Reflect on how the people in your life have influenced your personality, values or outlook over time.

4. How have your values shaped your journey? How does clarity around those values enrich your life?

5. Look at what's around you right now. Pick an item in your current sight you're grateful for and describe why.

6. What is something you often take for granted? What can you do to offer gratitude?

INTENTIONAL ACTIVATION

Gratitude Journal Prompts

7. I can show gratitude to my body, my vessel of life by _____.

8. When I am grateful, I feel _____.

9. A grateful heart allows me to _____.

10. I woke up this morning; that is a blessing because now I can experience _____ and for that I am grateful.

ABUNDANT WITH INTENTION

15
ELEVATE

ABUNDANT WITH INTENTION

ELEVATE

I elevate my life by choosing conscious thoughts that support my growth. With intentional awareness as my guide, I rise above self-doubt and align with purpose.

ELEVATE

With every breath, I choose to elevate my consciousness and connect to my higher self. This connection is my source of wisdom, clarity, and peace.

ELEVATE

I live with intentional energy to elevate my reality. Each action I take is rooted in my vision of a higher, more aligned life.

ELEVATE

I elevate my path by making the choice to let go of resistance and moving with intention. I am no longer reacting—I am consciously creating.

ELEVATE

I elevate my mind by trusting what inspires and expands the path before me. My thoughts are seeds, and I plant only those that grow into beauty and abundance.

ELEVATE

I trust my spirit will be elevated by nurturing stillness and presence within. In quiet, intuitive awareness, I hear divine guidance that leads to expansion intended for my journey.

ELEVATE

I elevate my experience of life with actions of faith over fear. I trust in the unseen and walk in alignment with my soul's purpose. This choice allows me to experience bountiful blessings.

ELEVATE

I trust the energy around me by being a conscious present. My awareness is elevated and transforms my life to tap into my highest power and divine purpose.

ELEVATE

Each intention I set helps elevate me to the highest version of myself. I live on purpose, and the Universe responds to my actions with endless opportunities specific to me.

ELEVATE

I elevate my vibration by tuning into gratitude, love, and truth. These high frequencies create space for miracles to unfold in my life.

ELEVATE

Through presence and awareness, I elevate my existence beyond old patterns. I release what no longer serves me and create from a place of inner power.

ELEVATE

I elevate my soul by listening to my internal voice and honoring my intuition and calling. Authenticity is my path, and I walk it with confidence and trust.

ELEVATE

I am awakened with a higher consciousness that elevates my existence. I align my intentions with purpose for the highest good. I open myself to the possibility of limitless abundance in all areas of my life.

ELEVATE

I elevate my journey by welcoming change with openness and courage. Each shift brings new possibilities that align with my highest good. I elevate my being by aligning my choices with love and truth.

ELEVATE

I elevate my journey by welcoming change with openness and courage. Each shift brings new possibilities that align with my highest good. I elevate my being by aligning my choices with love and truth.

ELEVATE

I am elevated in my reality by seeing each moment as a chance to grow. I am in my highest purpose when I meet life with curiosity, compassion, and clarity.

ELEVATE

I elevate the frequency of my life through deliberate thoughts and sacred action. I am here to rise, to expand, and to embody my fullest potential.

INTENTIONAL ACTIVATION

Saffron Mood Elixir

Saffron is a mood booster like no other. It has natural properties that influence brain chemistry, affecting neurotransmitters like dopamine, serotonin, and norepinephrine, that help regulate mood. I've been using saffron water in both the drink form, as well as to cook with and it's a game changer. But this month's home remedy takes it one step further! When you take a powerful herb like saffron, mix that with some ginger root and add a little pineapple for fun: you've got sunshine in the glass.

First step: Saffron Water. Take 1 tablespoon of saffron threads for 20 ounces of water,;soak them in the water for at least 30 minutes. Strain the threads and add one teaspoon of raw honey. You can store this in a mason jar in your refrigerator.
Second step: Mix 4 ounces of Saffron Water with 4 ounces of cold water
Third step: Peel and cut ginger root to 1/4 inch pieces to add to your water.
Fourth step: Add fresh chunks of pineapple, ice, and shake!

ABUNDANT WITH INTENTION

16

ABUNDANCE

ABUNDANT WITH INTENTION

ABUNDANCE

I choose abundance. I am worthy of abundance in all areas of life. My time, energy, and presence are valuable. I allow myself to receive without guilt or hesitation.

ABUNDANCE

I choose to give freely, knowing abundance returns to me tenfold. What I share with love and intentionality comes back in greater measure. Giving and receiving are part of the same beautiful flow of abundance.

ABUNDANCE

I choose to release a scarcity mindset and embrace abundance. My mind is a sacred ground for prosperity to grow. I speak and act from a place of abundance to manifest this into my reality.

ABUNDANCE

Today, I choose to live abundantly in thought, feeling, and action. I let go of fear and embrace the fullness of life. Abundance is here now, and I welcome it fully.

ABUNDANCE

I trust that what's for me will always find me. I genuinely celebrate the success of others, knowing abundance is infinite. There is no competition in true prosperity.

ABUNDANCE

I trust there is no limit to the abundance I can receive. The only limits are the ones I release now. I expand my consciousness into new levels of abundance with ease.

ABUNDANCE

I create abundance through passion and purpose. I trust my deep connection to the flow of universal abundance and prosperity.

ABUNDANCE

Each day, I align with the energy of abundance. I trust that abundance flows to me effortlessly and in perfect timing. I am open to receiving all the universe has to offer, knowing there are specific blessings for me.

ABUNDANCE

I live in a universe that is infinitely abundant. There is more than enough for everyone, including me. I align myself with the energy of limitless possibility.

ABUNDANCE

Every day, I attract more opportunities for growth and abundance. I recognize these openings and step into them confidently. My life expands as I do.

ABUNDANCE

My thoughts create an abundant reality. I align my values with intentions that support prosperity and success in meaningful ways.

ABUNDANCE

I am a magnet for abundance and success. I radiate confidence, trust, and gratitude. These qualities draw abundance to me naturally and intentionally.

ABUNDANCE

I am surrounded by abundance and prosperity. Everywhere I look, abundance multiplies in my favor. I simply choose to see and receive it in alignment with my highest good.

ABUNDANCE

I am grateful for the abundant blessings I already possess. From a place of gratitude, more abundance flows into my life.

ABUNDANCE

Abundance flows to and through me. I am open to receiving blessings in expected and unexpected ways. Prosperity is all around me, and I welcome it with grace.

ABUNDANCE

Abundance is my natural state. I do not chase it, I attract it. It comes to me because my energy and intentions align with it. I trust in its constant presence.

INTENTIONAL ACTIVATION

Choose Again Mindset is a method of conscious thought shifting and mindset adjustment to move from a state of lack or scarcity to a state of experiencing and attracting more abundance.

Awareness of blocks: Become conscious of any negative thoughts, beliefs, or patterns that are preventing you from experiencing abundance.

Choosing a different thought: When you notice a thought or feeling that aligns with scarcity or lack, you make a conscious choice to shift your focus to a thought that feels better or more aligned with abundance. This isn't about ignoring negative emotions, but rather creating a "perceptual shift".

Focusing on abundance: This helps to redirect your energy towards gratitude and positivity. When you actively look for abundance, you start to see more of it around you.

Building a belief system: By consistently choosing thoughts that align with abundance, you reinforce that belief and attract more positive experiences.

ONWARD
(CONCLUSION)

ABUNDANT WITH INTENTION

ONWARD (CONCLUSION)

If you made it here, you've either finished the sixteen affirmations that align with each of the sixteen intentions outlined in this book or you're taking a peek at the conclusion hoping that you can get a glimpse of what to expect if you read this book in its entirety. Either way, I'm glad you're here. This means you have made a deliberate choice to explore affirmations that connect you to different intentions on your path. You know what that is? That's living with intention. You have made a conscious choice. That's the first step. Everything starts with a choice.

Let's be very clear, this section is not a conclusion, but more of a reminder: there is no destination, regardless of the journey. This is simply a check-in point. This book is intended to be a companion on your journey, not a one-time read. It is my belief that as you progress on your journey, you will always need to set intentions as a practice to support living with intentionality because this is a lifestyle. Affirmations have always been my catalyst for that practice and something I'm honored to share with you.

You can use this book in its written chronological order, intention by intention, affirmation by

ONWARD (CONCLUSION)

affirmation or you can jump around and work with the affirmations that connect with you at the current time and your current intention. You have full agency to choose your path. Listen to your intuition and use these affirmations to serve your highest self. No one will know how to do that better than you.

These 16 intentions were a deliberate selection, not because they are the only intentions you can set. That would be ludacris to think we could capture the full human existence and cycle in the realm of sixteen intentions. But they are intended to support your journey in a universal and personal way by creating space in your practice and opening up your consciousness to the next level.

When you work with a specific intention, it's not the end, well, at least it's not intended to be. Intention setting builds muscle memory. When you are focusing on an intention, these affirmations can help support you in your current state and will adapt, as you will, for what you need when you revisit that intention again in the future. You'll be able to pull from your previous experience to connect with it on your terms.

ABUNDANT WITH INTENTION

As you commit to your intention setting practice, I hope you embrace all the authenticity that comes with it. I hope you embrace all of the wisdom that comes with it. And I hope you embrace all of the intention of your life in full alignment with your highest self. When we live with intention, we are not seeking or achieving perfection or a life with zero suffering. We are choosing to live a life in alignment with our values and we are trusting that the why of those values is intended to light up our path to our highest self.

Let's leave it with one last affirmation:

I choose to live with intention.
I trust my intentions are pure.
I support my intentions through deliberate actions that reflect my highest self.
I am intentional in all that I do.

BONUS MEDITATIONS

ABUNDANT WITH INTENTION

BONUS MEDITATION 1

I take this moment to silence the world around me. I am safe and secure. With each breath I take, I open my consciousness to connect with my intuition. My intuition speaks at the highest vibration and guides me on my intentional path.

I trust my intuition has the knowledge I need each step of the way. I am called to be intentional and deliberate. I am guided by a light within me.

(Visualize a light around your body, it will get brighter each time you repeat this phrase three times)

I am safe to live my life with the values I hold. I am worthy to live my life with the values I hold.

I trust that my values are designed with pure intentions and harmonious energy. I am in alignment with my intentions, I serve myself and the collective, like only I can.

(Place your hands on your heart, repeat this three times)

My actions are purposeful, I am intentional in all things.

My intentions are now one with my energy, and I use my energy for my highest potential.

BONUS MEDITATION 2

Your body is a vessel of peace and light. Root yourself to the Earth with a pure and deep connection.

Place your hand on the ground as an act of connection (Take three deep breaths in, exhale after each, and then pause)

Now place your hands on your heart as an act of connection (Take three deep breaths in, exhale after each, and then pause)

Again, place your hand on the ground as an act of connection (Take three deep breaths in, exhale after each, and then pause)

Now place your hands on your heart as an act of connection (Take three deep breaths in, exhale after each, and then pause)

Your intentions grow through purposeful action like the roots of a great oak tree. Visualize an oak tree, starting at the roots and slowly making your way to the top. Stay at the top for a moment and allow the sun to beam onto you. Feel the warmth. Hold gratitude for this moment.

In times of uncertainty, I rely on these roots. Keep your spirit grounded with the intentions that are planted in those strong roots. When you are in connection with the Earth, you are mindful and at peace.

Repeat to yourself: My energy is calm. My presence is strong. My mind is clear. My foundation is unbreakable.

BONUS MEDITATION 3

Allow yourself to slow down. Take this time to focus solely on your breath, drawing longer and longer breaths and pauses in a synchronistic fashion.

Close your eyes, if you feel comfortable enough to do so. (Or you can gaze off, starting at the tip of your nose)

Choose a place where you feel energetically connected. Be specific, take yourself there. Where are you? You are now sitting in this exact space.

Allow yourself the privilege to watch yourself from the outside, as if you are watching a friend, like an out-of-body experience. Watch yourself as you sit in silence, breathing deeply.

What do you feel?
What do you smell?
What do you hear?
What do you see around yourself?

Visualize yourself standing up, palms facing out to welcome the light of the universe in your space.

Witness yourself in all of your power.
Place your hands on your heart with gratitude to honor this experience.

BONUS MEDITATION 4

In this stillness, ask yourself quietly: "What can I let go of right now?" A thought? An expectation? A need to control?

Be as specific as you can. Visualize what you need to let go of, put it right in front of you. Now take a hold of it with your hands.
Physically, clinch your hands into fists, hold them as tightly as you can. Acknowledge the tensions that come with holding your first this tightly.

And when you are ready, open your hands and exhale audibly. Physically release the burden of what you are holding on.
Take a deep breath and feel the freedom that comes with surrender. Trust that even when you let go, you are held. You are supported. You are safe. Let this moment be enough. Let this breath be enough. Let go. And in this space of surrender, notice the peace that begins to rise in your physical body. Not from effort, but from simply allowing, simply being.

Take a few more slow, nourishing breaths.
Carry this softness with you and return to this practice when you feel called to.

Surrender is not the end, it is the beginning of peace.

ABUNDANT WITH INTENTION